Spiritual
SHORTCUTS

Spiritual
SHORTCUTS

7 Simple Keys to
Unlock Your Potential

Erin Wallace

O'LEARY
PUBLISHING
The Influencer's Press

NAPLES, FL

Published in the United States by
O'Leary Publishing
www.olearypublishing.com

The views, information, or opinions expressed in this book are solely those of the authors involved and do not necessarily represent those of O'Leary Publishing, LLC.

The author has made every effort possible to ensure the accuracy of the information presented in this book. However, the information herein is sold without warranty, either expressed or implied. Neither the author, publisher, nor any dealer or distributor of this book will be held liable for any damages caused either directly or indirectly by the instructions or information contained in this book. You are encouraged to seek professional advice before taking any action mentioned herein.

ISBN: 978-1-952491-98-6
ISBN: 978-1-952491-97-9
Cataloging-in-Publication Data is on file with the Library of Congress.

Developmental Editing by Heather Davis Desrocher
Line Editing by Kat Langenheim
Proofreading by Robert Gonzales
Illustrations by Jonathan Rambinintsoa
Cover and interior design by Jessica Angerstein
Printed in the United States of America

For those who have asked for help,
may this book be part of the answer!

Contents

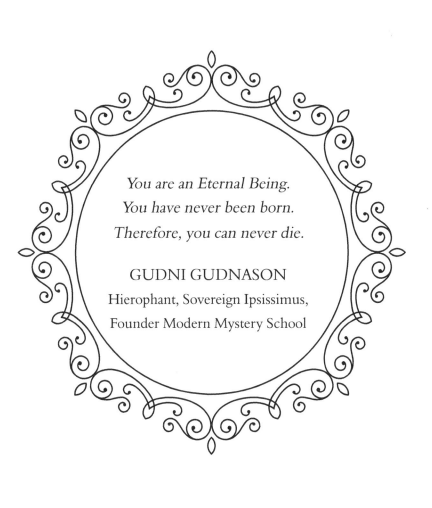

You are an Eternal Being.
You have never been born.
Therefore, you can never die.

GUDNI GUDNASON

Hierophant, Sovereign Ipsissimus,
Founder Modern Mystery School

Foreword

It is a great honour to write this foreword to *Spiritual Shortcuts*. As a guide, teacher and healer in the Modern Mystery School, and the Founder of Mini Me Yoga, my passion for supporting others through their progression has brought me so much joy, peace and healing. I believe that this book will support so many on the journey to become the very best version of themselves. The keys in this book will ignite the desire in you to live life fully and free of the things that weigh you down – ultimately leading to a more peaceful and fruitful life.

This book is a treasure map with wonderful golden nuggets of wisdom that are both practical and efficient. *Spiritual Shortcuts* will help you see things from a perspective that supports your evolution into the very best version of you.

I love how Erin makes these keys accessible to all. Both the beginner and the more advanced student of metaphysics and spirituality will gain practical tools from this little handbook.

This book is very timely, because it contains solutions to the issues that we face in modern life. Many people today avoid life and are easily offended, which creates separation. It does not have to be that way. In fact, if we are wise and have the right tools, we can use triggers to heal and become free.

Each chapter will guide you on the journey of self-discovery, to **Know Thyself**, and to heal the triggers that cause negative emotions. Erin helps us see how we can take our power back to change our lives in any way we want. This is HUGE!

Erin presents wisdom in a simple way that anyone can understand. Even better, she encourages you, the reader, to test out everything and discover what is true in your direct personal experience. Gaining this discernment and wisdom is the best way I have found to live the life of my dreams.

What a wonderful gift Erin has given us, in this inspiring handbook that can unlock your best life. She has done an amazing job of weaving her magick into this book, making it fun. In sharing her personal stories, you will benefit from the wisdom she has gained so you can climb the mountain of life more efficiently, and have fun while you do it.

Dr. Kate Bartram-Brown
Head of Modern Mystery School
UK & Europe

WARNING

Some of this material
may trigger you.

(But don't let that stop you!)

Metaphysics
A TURNING POINT

Have you ever asked yourself: *How do I know if the choices I am making in life are good ones?* Well, the best way I have found to answer that question is to look at the **fruits** that your choices produce. A healthy tree that receives care, water and anything else it needs produces fruit that is tasty, attractive and nutritious. We call this **good** fruit. The same is true in our lives. The results you experience tell you if you are making good choices. (Conversely, when our choices are not in alignment, we create results that are undesirable, or **bad** fruit.)

By their fruits you will know them.
Matthew 7:16

How do we find this discernment – this alignment – so we are not constantly hitting our head against the wall like a malfunctioning automatic vacuum? The answer to the question is found in the pages of this book, which shares shortcuts to streamline the process of discovery. The shortcuts will not take away the satisfaction of your efforts; they will act as a beacon so you can move forward in the light. You are meant to enjoy your experience here on Earth, and *Spiritual Shortcuts* will help you do just that.

Now, a shortcut does not mean that it is easy. A shortcut means that it is more efficient. (A shortcut is **not** a bypass.)

Imagine that you are hiking up a mountain. There are different ways to reach the top. You can take the switchbacks, which will be easier but will take longer; or, you can hike straight up the mountain (see the illustration), which may be harder, but you will arrive at the destination more quickly. You may even find a gondola that can take you up the mountain!

Life is the same way. You could *wander in the desert* for years – or use shortcuts to arrive at a life of joy, meaning, and abundance more quickly and efficiently. I know this is true, because I have used these shortcuts and experienced great results.

There was a time that I struggled and I was living in darkness. But the right book at the right time brought grace into my life, changing it dramatically and for good.

A person who has never made a mistake
has never tried anything new.
Albert Einstein

When I was in college, I had a traumatic experience. I was date raped. What made it especially traumatic was that I was a virgin at the time. I had wanted to wait to have sex until I fell in love, but that did not happen. I did not handle it well. It was during the time of AIDS and I was afraid I might die from having unprotected sex. Thankfully, I had a blood test and it was negative for HIV.

Even after my fear of death subsided, I still felt trauma from the violation. I was depressed; I smoked pot to cope with the loss of innocence. I had many negative thoughts. My world mirrored them, and I created a negative reality (we will go into how this works later). In turn, my negative reality gave me evidence that I should be upset. I then created even more negativity. It was a downward spiral that was hard to stop.

Enlightenment is when the wave
realizes it is the ocean.
–Thich Nhat Hanh

Over Christmas break, when I was home from college, I found a book that my mom had. It was called *Life is a Spiritual Experience: Metaphysics Made Practical,* by Paul. It was a very simple book on applied metaphysics that captured my attention and sparked my curiosity. It spoke to me.

The book talked about how thoughts are a higher vibration than the physical world, and that they come into the physical realm and manifest our reality. I tried the author's ideas for a month. One suggestion taught the importance of knowing that thoughts turn into matter, along with how to increase awareness of thoughts in order to actively create reality. This is the Hermetic principle of **"as above, so below."** I began to notice that controlling the quality of my thoughts was indeed shifting my material world. I was reminded that almost everything is energy; energy forms matter.

I became aware that I am the creator of my own world, and that I am responsible for what I attract and experience. I began to see everything through the lens of a teacher, and shifted my reality to an upward trajectory from applied metaphysics. I started to feel more positive and found more evidence that the world is good. I realized I am in control of my life and that I am **not** a victim. These realizations led me to change my entire focus from environmental studies (I was an environmental activist) to metaphysics.

I read everything I could find on metaphysics. I attended many workshops. Some of what was presented was New Age and did not have much power or truth behind it. I dabbled in some things that were super cool: a fire walk; a sweat lodge; studying healing with Barbara Brennan, author of *Hands of Light*; and exploring shamanism with Michael Harner, author of *The Way of the Shaman*. I then studied quantum physics with Dr. Amit Goswami, author of *The Self Aware Universe*, and learned how consciousness creates the material world. Dr. Goswami is also featured in the film *What the Bleep Do We Know*. His work helped me realize that everything I had already tested with metaphysics was actually proven with quantum physics. I was enthralled!

I also lived on a commune in the Rocky Mountains in Colorado, and met many spiritual teachers who lead workshops there. That exploration helped me develop discernment, which is the most important tool we can hone on our spiritual path.

So, reading *Life Is a Spiritual Experience* picked me up out of darkness and set me on a whole new path. Grace came into my life just when I needed it.

After completing a year and a half of Hellerwork training, which ended on the Gold Coast of Australia, I returned home and found the Modern Mystery School. The school changed my life in the most wonderful ways. The difference that the Modern Mystery School has over all the other paths I had explored was that it is **not** New Age. It has a lineage, which gives it more purity and power.

As I studied its teachings, I immediately felt their holiness, cleanliness, and sacredness. The school's ancient lineage comes from King Salomon, and before that from Hermes. It has been protected for those who are ready to progress and live as their God-selves – in the light. It is through my training in the Modern Mystery School that I gained the insights I will share with you.

Since that dramatic shift in my life began with a book, I have wanted to create a book that would help others find, or move along, their spiritual path more quickly. This is a handbook to living a life of joy, abundance, peace and love.

I hope that *Spiritual Shortcuts* will bring grace into your life. While there is no bypass in spiritual development, there are many paths that lead nowhere. This book offers tools that save time and angst, and are – in essence – shortcuts. May *Spiritual Shortcuts* do for you what Paul's book did for me.

So where do we start? I feel that the best shortcut I have experienced – and the key to life – is to **Know Thyself**. If you do not know yourself, your **real** self, you will create things that are not good for you or for others.

This is where we will start.

CHAPTER 1
Know Thyself

$\mathcal{A}$ bove the entrance to all the ancient mystery schools is written

Temet Nosce, or Know Thyself.

So, how do we come to know who we are? One place to turn for an answer is Hermetics, which is the foundation for most religions and philosophies in the world today. Hermes Trismegistus (called Hermes in Greece and Thoth in Egypt) explained the foundational laws of our reality in seven principles. These principles were used by the priests of Egypt, the philosophers of Greece, the creators of the Renaissance, and the revolutionaries of America. Hermetic means "secret" or "sealed."

The Hermetica says that the first sin (or error) is godlessness. What does godlessness mean? It means lack of awareness that you were made in the image of God and, therefore, are divine. We are the Gods of our own reality. The Hermetic principles are captured in various other written works, such as the Gnostic Bible, where Jesus says,

"Know ye not that ye are gods?"
–John 10:34

In most religions and spiritual communities, people do not feel comfortable identifying themselves as God. They might use the word source or universe, which dilutes the actual power of your true essence. I invite you to begin to see yourself as God – not the GOD, but the God of your own world – in your thoughts, actions, deeds. What does this look like? It looks like you creating your experience and your world.

You are more powerful than you know. Test this out. (You should test everything out, as your best guide is your direct personal experience.) When you have a really great day and everything goes well, it is likely because you created that with your thoughts. This then causes more positive thoughts, and then things go even better. Conversely, when you wake up on the *wrong side of the bed* and you stub your toe, then you are in a negative mood – and negative things happen. That causes your thoughts to be negative, which creates more negativity.

You are actually the cause in your world. Your thoughts are shifting the reality around you. To know who you are, the force of oneness, the God self, allows you to harness the power and use it. It allows you to align your will with God and create harmony, or heaven on earth. This happens through you, through me, through all of us.

All the problems we experience are because
we have forgotten we are Eternal Beings.
–Hideto Nakagome, Sovereign Ipsissimus
in the lineage of King Salomon

We have this unlimited potential that we have not even begun to tap into. We are programmed to believe that we are not God, and that we need to go through a priest to talk to God. We are taught that it is sacrilegious to say, "I am God." These false beliefs stop you from actually owning your own innate power. Even Jesus recognized us as God when he said,

All the things I've done,
ye shall do and more.
−John 14:12

THE 7 HERMETIC PRINCIPLES

Hermetics outlines seven principles that are the basis for much of our reality. You can use these principles to learn more about who you are (**Know Thyself**) and how the world works. In many ways they are the keys to the universe. They can empower you to live a more authentic and joyful life. I highly recommend that you read about them and find ways to apply them to your life. *The Kybalion* by Three Initiates is a great place to start. So what are The 7 Hermetic Principles?

Here they are:

1. MENTALISM The All is Mind; The Universe is Mental.

2. CORRESPONDENCE As Above, so Below; As Within, so Without.

3. VIBRATION Nothing Rests, Everything Moves; Everything Vibrates.

4. POLARITY Everything is Dual and has poles or opposites.

5. RHYTHM Everything Flows, Out and In; Everything has its Tides.

6. CAUSE AND EFFECT Every Cause has its Effect; every Effect has its Cause.

7. GENDER Gender is in everything; Everything has its Masculine and Feminine Principles.

As a way to spark your interest, I will share one Hermetic Principle at the end of each chapter based on which one most closely aligns with the topic of that chapter.

*Hermetics is the understanding of what
allows light to exist within your life.*

Dave Lanyon, Sovereign Ipsissimus
in the Lineage of King Salomon

RESPONSIBILITY EQUALS POWER

Another way to **Know Thyself as Divine** is to take full responsibility for your life. This includes no longer blaming
others. You cannot be God and a victim at the same time.
When you take responsibility, you are honoring that God
power that you have. When you are a victim, you are still a
God, but you are not taking responsibility so you cannot shift
the situation.

When you realize that you are responsible for things going poorly, then you also realize that you are responsible for
things going well. Knowing that you have that power helps
you to harness and use it. If your life has not gone well, you
created that and you could take responsibility for it and say,
*Wow, I'm so powerful that I (unknowingly) created this poor life for
myself. Now, what life do I want to create?*

As we come to truly **Know Thyself** we become aware not only of our strengths, but also our weaknesses. These blocks and triggers take us away from our power; and therefore, we want to find them so we can remove or heal them. That is what we will look at in the next chapter.

If you would like to go deeper with the principles in this chapter see the appendix for practical exercises.

"We were born to make manifest the
glory of God that is within us."
Marianne Williamson

THE 7 HERMETIC PRINCIPLES

The Principle of Correspondence

As above, so below;

As below, so above;

As within, so without.

There are planes that we can understand through looking at the plane we are in.

We can shift the outer by shifting the inner.

Consider where you see this principle in your life. How can you use this principle to help you as you navigate life?

CHAPTER 2
FIND YOUR BUTTONS

Your issues and triggers are totally unique to *you*. Have you ever noticed that some people are not as bothered by certain things as you are? This is because your triggers or issues come from specific, painful experiences in *your* life. Now, because we are the Gods or Creators of our world, we can create anything; but we create from our beliefs. If our beliefs are based on wounds, we will not create good fruits in our life. When something painful happens, you can be wounded. That wound, if left unhealed, will become a part of you and create a belief about the way the world works. It may not be true in reality, but in your world it becomes law. Your belief then attracts more of the same, and so the cycle goes. Your wounds and your triggers hold you back from your best life.

You might have a certain pattern around relationships or money (these are the two most common areas where people struggle.) This means you keep entering into poor relationships or you are always running out of money. What do all those situations have in common? The answer is *you*. It might be a hard pill to swallow to realize that you are doing this to yourself.

AS WITHIN SO WITHOUT

The outer world is a reflection of the inner world. When we clean up the pollution in our inner world, we will see pollution disappear in the outer world. When we end the war within us, we will find peace in the world. As within, so without. If you want peace and a clean environment in the world, create it within you first.

Our subconscious mind and our ego stop us from the life we want to live. Let's say you have an experience too painful for you to face at the moment. You might push it down, but it is in your subconscious, and like a buoy it is going to come up. In this case it comes up in your outer world.

To find your triggers, it helps to understand how energy works. Whatever is in our energy field will attract more things like it to itself. There is a pattern or an energetic signature to every trigger – like a red button. And until those triggers are healed, people or situations will continue to come into your life to push your buttons so you can see and heal them.

Finding your buttons
gives you the power.

Some words, like God, may trigger you due to religious programming, for example. Find all the things that trigger you. (Things I say in this book will likely trigger you - use that to help you!) The reason it is beneficial to be aware of your triggers is because they act as magnets to draw situations that match the energy of the trigger *until* you have healed and cleared the cause. For example, you believe you will be cheated on because you were once cheated on. This belief creates a magnet for more of the same experience!

There is an easy way to see if a button from the past has been pushed. If somebody says something that offends you or upsets you, talk about it with a trusted friend. If you are not able to clear it after 15 minutes, then there is something from the past that has been triggered, and it is keeping you from freedom. If you set your boundary, state your needs or wants, and move on, then you know it is not a trigger. You can be strong in many areas of your life, but if as soon as your button is pushed you collapse like a house of bricks, you still have unresolved triggers. The goal is to clear yourself until you are trigger free. How do we find our buttons? Well, of course, other people will show them to us!

BRING IN THE LIGHT

Another way to find our buttons is to bring in light to illuminate our triggers and blocks. When we bring in light, we can see the situation more clearly and understand the beliefs that hold us back.

What is the light? The light is spiritual, but we can understand it from studying physical light. Imagine you spend a week at a vacation rental. When you arrive, it is dark, and you imagine how clean it is.

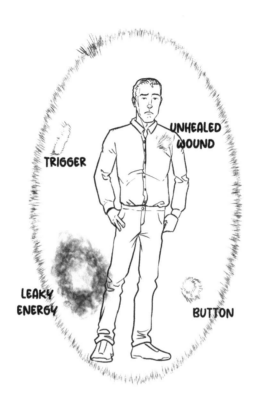

Then you turn on the light and see cobwebs in the corners, and maybe a spot on the mirror. The light shows you the things that need to be cleaned. Spiritual light does the same thing. It shines on our beliefs and patterns of behavior and thought. Once we are aware of them, we can work to heal them.

In the vacation rental, the light might also show great things about the space – like the quality of the furniture and all of the amenities. Spiritual light will show your beautiful beliefs and patterns as well.

You are like a house. Maybe the first floor looks great, but when you go into the basement and turn on the light you may see old boxes of stored papers and other items. These represent subconscious baggage that has yet to be unpacked. You would not even see the baggage if it was not for the light. Each box represents a trigger of which you are unaware until something or someone triggers you. The best way I have found to start shining spiritual light on yourself is through a Life Activation, which I will explain in more detail later in the book.

Activations, healings and Initiations
are essential to your progression as a human.
Dave Lanyon, Sovereign Ipsissimus

I love the light because it shows us the beliefs that are running our lives. Once we see them, we can choose to let them stay, or remove them. We can ask, *Do I still want to believe this about the world?* Then at least we are consciously choosing our beliefs, which is more empowering than letting unconscious beliefs run our lives.

When we shine spiritual light on ourselves, we may find beliefs such as: *money is evil, all brunettes will break up with me, or I need to struggle to succeed.* The examples are endless.

*What false beliefs
are holding you back?*

It can be unpleasant to become aware of the beliefs that have been running your life. But it is only temporary. Seeing and removing them, which we will address in Chapter 3, will save you a lot of pain in the future. Train yourself to *see the gold* in every trigger. This is how I now live my life, and it has brought me wonderful results.

WALKING THE TALK

Let me share how this *seeing the gold* works in my life. I am an initiate, Teacher and Guide with The Modern Mystery

School, which offers me so many beautiful ways to apply my gifts, as well as to understand the beliefs and triggers that hold me back. Over the last 17 years, I have grown so much. I went from reluctantly offering meditation classes – I felt unworthy and awkward within myself – to then becoming a Guide and teaching Empower Thyself. Eventually I trained to teach a large 5-day class called Healer's Academy. I have even become a Universal Hermetic Ray Kabbalah Instructor who teaches around the world.

Standing in front of a class of students can push my buttons, show me my wounds, and illuminate my false beliefs or emotional attachments. I was so uncomfortable each time this happened that I was motivated to clear the triggers and heal. There is nothing more frightening than freezing in front of a group of people – especially when they are your students.

Each time this happened, I would go home and seek out healing for each wound that was revealed. Each time I did this, it became easier because there were fewer triggers! I was going into deep layers pulling triggers out by the root.

Recently, I served on the Healer's Academy panel as a teacher; and I was amazed at the ease I experienced teaching at this international program. And then I found one hidden, lingering issue. I discovered that when I am onstage with other panel members, but not talking or teaching, I have a somatic panic response. How did I respond to this? I thought, *Cool! I just found something else I can heal.* I am so grateful – life just keeps getting better and better the more I do this!

When you work to clear a trigger, you can test it to see if it still bothers you. Maybe you won't attract those triggering situations or people anymore. When you are no longer triggered, you can now use all that energy for something good.

The human mind is too busy energetically
to appreciate the true subtleties
of spiritual reality without proper
metaphysical training.

Dr. Ann Donnely, Council of 12,
Modern Mystery School

The key is to constantly challenge yourself – sort of like a bodybuilder must find new exercises to keep progressing.

The Modern Mystery School and the Lineage of King Salomon has helped me leap exponentially – and I highly recommend this path if you want to leap to your best life!

CAUTION, BEWARE

In today's society, many people police the outside world to avoid being triggered or they avoid people who trigger them. Is this true freedom? No, it is weakness. When we blame others for our situation, we are not free. When we are offended or triggered, we give up our power. That is never going to help us live a life of freedom. We must clear the triggers inside of us so that nothing on the outside can rob us of our energy or peace. Then we are truly free.

Any energy you use to police others is wasted. That same energy could be used toward manifesting your goals, creating peace on earth, and using your gifts. Other people will push your buttons; but it is your responsibility to remove the button so it can no longer be pushed. Once we become aware of these patterns, we can shift. If you have the blessing of discovering a trigger, then you can work on it to heal the wound. You can go back in time through meditation and shift your belief or understanding of what happened.

When you pay more attention to what is triggering you versus who is triggering you, your healing journey begins.
Tory Eletto

Yes, there are things that others do that are unacceptable. But, we cannot control others, as much as we may wish we could. But we can control ourselves and our reactions. There are cases where we need protection or help; but most of the time, we just need to focus on removing our buttons so they can no longer be pushed.

There are many examples of two people in the same situation – maybe even in the same family – who end up living very different lives. They have experienced the same upbringing, and yet one becomes successful while the other does not. The difference is that one chooses to live as a God, while the other chooses to live as a victim. Which one do you want to be?

If you would like to go deeper with the principles in this chapter see the appendix for practical exercises.

THE 7 HERMETIC PRINCIPLES

The Principle of Cause & Effect

Every cause has its effect;
every effect has its cause;
everything happens according to law;
chance is but a name for a law not recognized.
There are many planes of causation but nothing escapes the law.
You can master this law by obeying the causation
of the higher planes so you can rule the plane you are on.
Become a chess player rather than a pawn.

Consider where you see this principle in your life. How can you use this principle to help you as you navigate life?

CHAPTER 3

FREE YOURSELF

Healing our wounds and clearing our triggers allows us freedom to live a life of joy and abundance. This is not easy or pleasant work, but it is so worth it. One way I have inspired myself to do the work of healing my wounds is to look to spiritual masters. Who in the world today, or throughout history, inspires you? Maybe one of these figures: Joan of Arc, Martin Luther King Jr., Mother Teresa, Gandhi, or Jesus.

For many, the ultimate one who shows us the way is the Buddha. How did the Buddha become enlightened? He let go of all of his triggers and attachments, so nothing bothered him. Nothing could catch him because there were no magnets or leaks in his energy field. His ability to remain detached from triggers inspires me. I want to live life as the Buddah did. The goal is to clear yourself until you are trigger free!

The Buddah has no buttons, no magnets for anything to affect him, so the arrows bounce off like water off a duck's back!

So how do we heal our triggers? I am happy I can share this with you as it took me a long time to figure it out. Your triggers or buttons come from hurt or trauma in your childhood. It could be something as simple as someone looked at you the wrong way, or something more serious such as sexual or emotional abuse. It all affects you, but you do not need to carry these wounds from the past any longer.

Your wounded child is your responsibility,
and that is a blessing –
because you can give yourself
the love you didn't receive.

When we identify the trigger or the lead, you can turn this lead into *gold*. When you feel triggered, ask yourself: How old do I feel at this moment? If the answer is anything other than your current age, don't shy away from looking deeper! Go within and trace that triggered feeling, all the way back to the first time. See the child you were back then. Comfort and love him or her. Let your younger self know that you will be there for him or her. This can be easier said than done, and sometimes inner child healing needs to be practiced repeatedly.

Your parents had their own wounds from their family. Who knows what kind of beliefs or dysfunctions were passed onto them through your lineage. While you can forgive them, it does not take away the fact that your needs were not met, and you were hurt. But now *you* can heal that. The good news is *you* can become the perfect parent to your younger self.

Only you can heal your inner child. Someone else might try to heal your child, but it will not work. Most people have not yet done this work themselves, so how can another wounded child look after your wounded inner child?

When we are children we cannot escape our family, and we need to think of creative ways to survive. But as adults, we have to look at the strategies we used for survival and see if they are still of use to us or if they need to be healed.

Our relationships with our siblings can be one of the places with opportunities for growth. You may know what I am talking about! One of the childhood issues I have worked on is my relationship with my older sister. I was the second child, and I felt like my sister resented that I came into the family dynamic. Our perceptions are often incorrect, but to us they are often truth. I was a sensitive child and so feeling this, I dimmed my light and let her take center stage.

There were some benefits to staying in the background – I could observe more and was shielded in some ways by her and the dynamic, but for the most part this was an unnatural coping mechanism. Also, she had never asked for this adjustment; it was just something my child logic came up with as a solution. I kept this approach in the family dynamic well into my adult life. Luckily, I did not bring this into my friend group. There I had a lot of friends and allowed myself to shine.

Until you make the unconscious conscious,
it will direct you and you will call it fate.
~ Carl Jung

As an adult, I was able to finally shift this dynamic even in my family. One Thanksgiving, we were going around the table saying what we were thankful for, and as I began to talk, some of my family members began a conversation, totally ignoring me. I was able to see that I had created a pattern of being ignored in my family as a coping mechanism. Instead of blaming them or becoming angry, I paused and thought about how I could heal this pattern within myself.

I excused myself and went into the back room to meditate. I found my ignored inner child in the "basement" and I consoled her. By Christmas, the pattern had totally shifted – everyone asked me about life with interest. The funny thing was that I did not even feel the need for that attention anymore: I was good with myself.

This is the sort of shift you can look forward to as you do this work!
We abandon ourselves when we:

- Ignore our inner voice
- Chase love
- Fix, rescue, save, caretake
- Prioritize others needs above our own
- Betray ourselves to be chosen
- Say yes when we want to say no
- Explain away or ignore red flags
- Give 2nd, 3rd, 4th chances
- Allow abusive behavior

As traumatized children we dreamed that someone would come to save us, we never dreamed that it would, in fact, be ourselves as adults.

As we clear false beliefs and remove our buttons or triggers, we become our true selves. Our goal is to **Know Thyself** and to live authentically as who we truly are.

PRACTICAL SUGGESTIONS

I recommend receiving a Life Activation to jump start this process. The session will infuse light into your physical and spiritual DNA and illuminate your God given gifts; it will also show you things that need to be healed or cleared. There are practitioners all over the world. You could also take a class called Empower Thyself that will give you rituals that put a container of light around you. This protects you, and also helps show you what is blocking you.

Take responsibility
for the world.

HO'OPONOPONO

One technique that you can use right away is the Hawaiian Method of clearing. The premise is that we create our own reality; and if something is in our world then it is a part of us. So, we must take responsibility for it – no exceptions.

There is a miraculous story of Dr. Ihaleakala Hew Len who learned a technique from *Morrnah Simeona*. This is an ancient method of taking responsibility for the world around us, and clearing it from within ourselves.

Dr. Hew Len says that Ho'oponopono is the process where we say to The Divine:

"I love you." (unification)

"I'm sorry." (repentance)

"Please forgive me." (forgiveness)

"Thank you." (transmutation)

If you see something you do not like, it is in you and you can clear it by using this method. We know that saying these words can shift things. Dr. Hew Len used this practice at a high security facility for the mentally insane who had all committed heinous crimes. Over a period of a few months, he sat with the chart of each patient everyday and said the Ho'oponopono. He did not interact with the patients in a clinical sense, but viewed their files and felt what came up for him as he reviewed the files. He repeated the above mantra to clear whatever was in *himself*. Things shifted within the institution and within a few years all the inmates were released.

The Ho'oponopono teaches that taking 100% responsibility for everything you see, feel, and experience is the way to live your best life.

PRACTICAL APPLICATION

A key to finding your hidden subconscious blocks or weaknesses is to watch who makes you react. Is there someone in your life who just irks you or who you think about negatively? Who do you complain about to your friends or co-workers? Please make a list of the qualities this person possesses that bother you (before reading ahead).

Go ahead and write this down.

Now, the big reveal – this person is doing something that *you* do but have not accepted or cannot see. This person is a mirror of you! Pretty confrontational, right? You want to deny it – your negative ego doesn't want to admit it. I know because I have been there. Keep looking until you find it. Sometimes it is not so obvious. You may wonder: *what about someone who abuses children? How am I like them?* Well, do you ever beat up on yourself or your inner child?

You can use the mantra above to heal this. Also, simply being aware of it will help you to integrate and accept that part of yourself; and you will find yourself neutral to the exact same person who used to bug you so much!

Pretty incredible!!!

If you would like to go deeper with the principles in this chapter see the appendix for practical exercises.

THE 7 HERMETIC PRINCIPLES

The Principle of Polarity

Everything is dual;
everything has poles;
everything has its pair of opposites;
like and unlike are the same;
opposites are identical in nature but different in degree
(hot and cold, light and dark).
Extremes meet;
all Truths are but Half-Truths;
All Paradoxes may be reconciled
If you experience the negative,
it means you can experience the positive.

Consider where you see this principle in your life. How can you use this principle to help you as you navigate life?

CHAPTER 4

BE AUTHENTIC

When we were children in a family unit, we used different coping mechanisms to survive. Sometimes through religion or our schooling, we were programmed to believe certain things. The belief systems or prejudices of our parents and our friends often led us to create a false self so that we would receive love from them. This false self covered up our individuality and true self.

This false self can be thought of as masks that we have worn. These masks cover up who we really are; and when we wear a mask for many years we may come to believe that the mask is who we are. There comes a time when we may realize that these masks no longer serve us and it is time to remove them.

As we come to know our true selves, we may have to learn how to express ourselves in the world authentically. A lot of times we don't even know how *we* feel because we do not have boundaries with those in our lives. If you have learned to ignore your feelings to survive, you might not even realize when you are upset about something another person does until hours or days later.

Since you did not realize their actions bothered you, you did not tell them and you did not set a boundary with them. And then the person does the same thing a second time. You haven't told them your expectations because you don't even know your own expectations. The second time, you might understand that you are upset more quickly. But not soon enough to say anything. So, then the person does it again – without knowing that it is an issue for you. And this time you blow up.

For example, you are meeting a friend for coffee and she is late. It does not feel good, but you do not realize what the issue is for a few days. So you do not let your friend know that her lateness is an issue. She comes late a second time. But again, you are not really aware that it bothers you as much as it does. The third time your friend is late to meet you, your annoyance has built up to the point that you get angry and blow up. And then your friend may think, *Why is she upset? I don't have any idea what upsets her.* If you do not know how you feel, or cannot set boundaries or expectations, you become an unsafe person for those around you.

To shift this pattern, get into your body and be present. You will be able to identify in the moment if something is bothering you. (Rolfing or Hellerwork can help you get into your body so that you actually know how you feel.) It is like, when as a child someone steals your lollipop and you say, "Hey, I don't like that. Don't take my lollipop. I want it back." And then you move on with your life. You don't talk about it with your friends or process it over and over. You just move on. That's an example of being healthy.

When we are clear with others about our expectations and our boundaries, it makes life much clearer. Sometimes people aren't used to someone setting a boundary in the moment and then moving on, so they might think it's harsh. But it is authentic, and in the long run they will actually trust you more. They could decide to agree with that or not. And you could decide if you want to hang out with them or not – no harm, no foul. Authenticity and clarity save a lot of angst and confusion in relationships with others.

As I came to know myself better and committed to living authentically in all areas of my life I made a promise to myself.

Do not do ANYTHING
that you do not want to do.
(Unless it is in service.)

This means that when I am sharing a meal with a friend, or I am talking to someone on the phone, I am doing it because I want to. And everyone feels this difference. My friends and family all know that if I am with them, it is because I want to be with them. This feels good to others.

Another way to be authentic is to be in tune with the Hermetic Principle of Rhythm, which is about the ebb and flow of things. There is an ebb and flow to everything: like the waves on a beach, the tide and the moon cycles, and even the cycles of the year. Sometimes your body or energy needs solitude where you can go within, and sometimes you are up for going out. Knowing your own rhythms will support you here.

Consider this: you are invited to a party; you do not really want to go but you go anyway. Or you do not want to speak to someone who calls you, but you just muddle your way through the conversation. In both situations you are not really present and you end up being resentful. That is not good for either of you.

Let us say that your friend asks you to hang out when you don't want to, but you feel badly or think you should, so you do. That is actually not kind. I would never want someone to hang out with me if that is not really what they wanted to do. I would rather my friend tell me the truth that he or she wants to be alone.

This does come with a caveat. Sometimes when we say *no* we are actually avoiding discomfort. For example, if you do not want to go to a party, is it because you have social anxiety? Is there something that scares you? If this is true, then you need to look at it through a different lens, and work to heal what is causing you to avoid something.

But if you genuinely do not want to talk to someone, or genuinely do not want to go to the party, then don't. Now you are preserving your integrity and you become someone people can trust. They know that if you're talking to them, it is because you enjoy it. They know if you say something, you mean it. And if you don't say something, they know that you're okay. They do not have to second guess you or read your mind. This is authenticity.

REMOVING THE MASK

We can wear different masks to cover up our real emotions. I wore a mask of happiness all of the time – a fake smile. Even when I was uncomfortable, scared or angry, I wore a happy mask. Others might appear tough to protect an inner sensitivity or joke around to cover up discomfort.

These masks served a purpose. But as adults we are not stuck in our family dynamic – we can move away from situations that do not work for us. Even if you do not have resources, you can walk or ride a bike to move away. We are no longer stuck even if the mind thinks we are.

I remember in junior high thinking, *Oh my gosh, if I don't have friends, I am going to die.* When we were young our brain was not developed and we had limited life experience. We might have thought that little things were the end of the world. As we grew older, if we kept these outdated beliefs and coping mechanisms we limited our expansion and progression.

The first step is to identify your masks so you can decide if you want to keep them. Taking masks off will help you exist in the moment, perceiving what is actually going on in front of you, instead of projecting a memory from the past or a fear of the future.

When we do the work of healing,
and repairing our filters, our mind, and our soul,
we will then automatically begin to manifest
more of the Divine Light that flows from source.

Dr. Theresa Bullard, Ipsissimus in the Lineage of King Salomon

The masks we wear come from places where we may have been hurt. And these masks distort how we see others because we look at each other through the lens of our wounds.

We do not see each other authentically. Instead we (unconsciously) say things like, *Oh, you're the teacher from third grade who was mean to me. You are the person who broke up with me. You are the friend who ditched me.* But none of this is true in the present. And then we wonder why our relationships have drama in them.

When you have freed yourself of your buttons and removed your masks, you will live more easily in the present moment. Then you can enjoy the beauty in front of you, and the unlimited possibilities all around you. You will experience a range of emotions based on living in the present, which is a more joyful way to experience life.

We don't see things as they are,
we see things as we are.
—Anais Nin

UNIVERSAL HERMETIC RAY KABBALAH

When I first heard about Kabbalah I knew nothing about it, except that Madonna was into it. I was a second step initiate in the Lineage of King Salomon, which means I had done Empower Thyself and gone to Healer's Academy. I was taking my first class with Founder Gudni Gudnason to start my training as a Ritual Master, which is the path of the Warrior. This includes working to eliminate the negative ego, the part of you that can be triggered, and that has beliefs from the past that cause you to project onto others. The negative ego is the part that keeps us small! I asked Founder Gudni, "How can I start working on this?" He answered, "Do the King Salomon Healing Modality and take Kabbalah."

Luckily there was a Kabbalah class starting in LA, and I signed up – not knowing what it was, but knowing that I had to be there. I remember driving down from San Francisco and feeling absolutely terrified. All my fears came up strong the night before. When I walked into the room, most people there looked like actors and models, and I immediately regressed to the 7th grader who had braces and acne and no one with whom to eat lunch. In reality, my subconscious patterns that I carried with me were projecting themselves. Why was this happening as I stepped into the first day of Kabbalah class? Well, I now know that the Tree of Life (see illustration) is a mechanism that will bring to light aspects of yourself that need clearing.

By day two, everything had shifted for me. I came back to class and the teacher, Theresa Bullard, PhD (the host of Mystery Teachings on Gaia TV) asked me to teach part of the class! The people who looked like models asked me to be their study partners, and people wanted to sit with me at lunch. All of a sudden, the old pattern had shattered; and I could see that I was not in 7th grade, but actually a vibrant and attractive 30 year old. This is even before the real process began! Miraculous!

From personal experience I know that one of the best ways to remove masks and be authentic is through the Universal Hermetic Ray Kabbalah Ascension program. Ascending the Tree of Life in a Kabbalah will clear your subconscious patterns and help you strengthen your Divine Gifts. The Kabbalah experience is a potent and direct way to freedom – you could say it is a *shortcut* right up the mountain.

The illustration on the next page is the tree of life, and each sphere or circle is called a Sephirah, which is an aspect of our divine self. Each sphere contains vices and virtues. As we ascend the tree from the bottom (earth or the physical world) to the top (crown or spirit or God) we are releasing triggers, beliefs, and subconscious patterning, and strengthening our soul body, which connects our spirit to our physical body. This, in turn, allows us to connect with the will of God more readily and infuse that light and goodness into our choices and manifestations on earth. These aspects of God within us are there all the time.

THE TREE OF LIFE

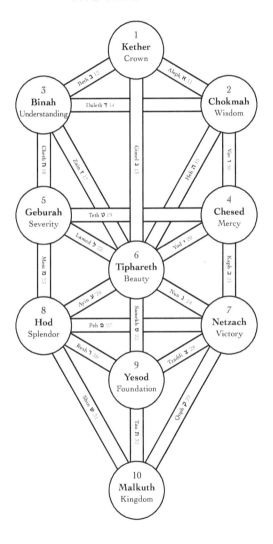

Within the Tree of Life we see two important Hermetic Principles. First, we see the Hermetic Principle of Gender. There is a masculine pillar on the right that is about force (energy moving outward and expansion), and a feminine pillar on the left that is about form (a container for creation that not only restricts but also defines). The feminine and masculine energies are each needed for creation – just like life is created biologically with a male and a female.

One aim in the alchemical process of ascending the Tree of Life is to find balance between the two pillars so we are on the middle pillar. This is like functioning at the center of a wheel – while life is spinning around you, you can remain calm in the center of yourself. We all have a middle pillar within us (the peaceful witness self) and we can always find it.

Second, we see the principle of polarity on the tree in the masculine and feminine, Power and Love, Intellect and Emotion. Just like hot and cold, they are the same on a continuum – but different in degree.

Kabbalah is the holy study of the God Essence within humans and helps us to align with the will of God. In the next chapter we will explore how to align with the will of God!

If you would like to go deeper with the principles in this chapter see the appendix for practical exercises.

THE 7 HERMETIC PRINCIPLES

The Principle of Rhythm

Everything flows, out and in;
everything has its tides;
all things rise and fall;
the pendulum-swing manifests in everything.
How far the pendulum swings to one side,
is the same amount it will swing to the other side.

Consider where you see this principle in your life. How can you use this principle to help you as you navigate life?

CHAPTER 5

ALIGN WITH THE WILL OF GOD

At the beginning of my journey, I spent so much time and money searching for the answers without feeling much progress. The truth is, it doesn't have to be that hard. We are on this journey back to our Divinity together, so when I help you I also help me. When I help me I also help you. We are all one and cannot have Shamballah (peace or heaven on Earth) until we are all there! I do not want to be at the party all by myself, so I wanted to share some of the gems I have discovered. This next one is so simple yet so powerful!

You can find a way to freedom more quickly
by aligning with the will of God.

What is the will of God? The *will of God* is a desire that is aligned with the good of all. You receive something that benefits others. Usually we desire and manifest while focusing on just our own self or our own separate body. We think we are separate and we need to compete with others. We are in survival mode, protecting our interests. We see the view from the ground.

But when we rise up and see the larger picture we see a beautiful pattern from above. The truth is that we are all connected – we are all in this together – and we are one. When we align with the will of God, we are choosing something that is going to help others too. We can still have our desires and our goals to move forward in our lives, but when we align these desires with the will of God they have more power and purity.

Let us say you desire something and want to manifest it. Try sitting quietly and connect to whatever it is that gives you a higher perspective. Maybe think of a pyramid or a triangle, which in Sacred Geometry has the energy of spirit. Then to align your desire with the will of God (the good of all), say, "I desire this in alignment with the highest good of all. This or something better." Always ask for your actions and words to be in alignment with the will of God. If you raise whatever it is that you want up to spirit, you will have more power to achieve it.

What does it mean to align with the will of God? It means that as a God on earth, you are creating good and bringing in light. You pull down from the mind of God and are there to support the good of humanity, the progression of yourself and others. You become united with your brothers and sisters.

Maybe you have never realized that you are a God on earth. Imagine what you can create in your life and for the world if you live and act as an expression and embodiment of the Divine.

When we identify just as our body or personality (which is based on the wounds that we have gathered in our physical existence) we are not aligned with the will of God. When we are focused on the things that have happened to us, or are acting based on our negative programming, we are not bringing in good. We are acting from the false self – the negative ego. When we let the negative ego take over, we are going to create things that are not for the good of all, or even for our true self. We will create bad fruit and will have a karmic debt to pay. I am sure you can find some times from your past when this happened.

As you begin to align with the will of God, you will continue to work on knowing yourself deeply and authentically. Spirituality is a cycle. When you come to know yourself more deeply, you align better with the will of God, which leads to knowing yourself better. It is a continual deepening.

HAWAII

Here is an example of how I could align my desires with the will of God. I am obsessed with Hawaii, and always want to go there. One way to go would be to focus on myself and not do anything that would help other people. But if I set the intention to go in alignment with the will of God, it will be easier for me to manifest the trip because now it will serve more people. Maybe I will sit next to someone on the airplane who needs to hear what I have to share about a teaching or a healing. Maybe I can lift their spirits.

Maybe I will stay in a VRBO or Airbnb that has some weird energy. Maybe the owners have had a hard time renting it, or want better reviews, and have prayed for a solution.

Since I am trained to do house clearings, I can clear the space using sage, sacred geometry, and the ancient prayers that I have learned in order to help the owners and all those who stay there in the future – which is something I do wherever I stay. Once, when I was in Hawaii, I visited a sacred site that needed a little bit of a boost. I did some rituals there and left it better energetically than how I found it.

In this way, I have my trip to Hawaii, but I am also supporting other people at the same time. I live this way when I teach. I pray that my word and actions are in alignment with the will of God, that way I know that what I say will serve the students in their progression. I have made this prayer in writing this book as well. This is what it looks like to align with the will of God.

If you are not aligning with the will of God you are using your powers to create more negativity in the world. We always want to focus on the progression of humans in the light, which is staying in alignment with the will of God. This will bring you more and more of what you want.

One way to test if you are in alignment with the will of God is by the fruits of your choices and actions. Good fruits will show you that you are in alignment.

WIN/WIN

Another guideline to ensure you are aligned with the will of God is to only enter into agreements or relationships where both parties win. This is not the politically correct trend of 'everyone wins' in sports or challenges, or the trend of everyone receiving an award. This means each person benefits from the energy exchange within an agreement. Examples are: someone working for you feels fairly compensated for their time; or you and a friend are going on a trip and your friend loves to drive, so you are happy to be the passenger. In all things, make it a win/win. It is possible to do this.

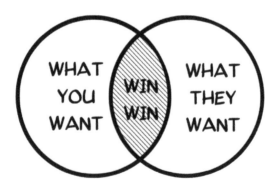

Another important law or rule is the Golden Rule that states 'do unto others as you would have done to yourself' or 'do unto others as they would have you do.' This takes the Win/Win guideline a step further by considering that we all have different desires and preferences, and it is helpful to know them.

Win/Win is a kind and clean way to move through the world as everyone really is us – we are one. What we do onto another, we are actually doing to ourselves. Our motivation should not be fear, even though it is true that what we reap we sow.

The definition of evil is anything
that stops someone's progression in the light.

The Golden Rule is found in every religion.

Hinduism – Everything you should do, you will find in this: *Do nothing to others that would hurt you if it were done to you.*

Buddhism – Do not offend others as you would not want to be offended.

Taoism – The successes of your neighbor and their losses will be to you as if they were your own.

Judaism – That which you do not wish for yourself you shall not wish for your neighbor. This is the whole law. The rest is only commentary. *Talmud Shabbat 31*

Christianity – In everything, do to others what you would have them do to you. For this sums up the law and the prophets. *Matthew 7:12*

Islam – None of you shall be true believers unless you wish for your brother the same that you wish for yourself. *Summajt*

Confucianism – Is there any rule that one should follow all of one's life? Yes! The rule of gentle goodness. That which we do not wish to be done to you, we do not do to others. Analectas 15:33

If you realize what you have done to another,
you do to yourself, you will have
understood a great truth.

Lao Tzu

Here is a timely example of how to use the Golden Rule. Recently, something HH the Dalai Lama said to a child was taken out of context. A spliced video went viral and people on social media immediately condemned him without understanding the whole situation. There is a different way of being in Tibet, and what he had said was completely innocent. But to some outsiders who do not understand Tibetin culture, his words seemed wrong and they publicly criticized him for what he had said.

It is very easy to judge others, but the best thing to do is to focus on understanding what is really happening on a deeper level. There is so much that we do not know or understand, and when we have the full picture of something, it may look very different than we originally thought. Give people the benefit of the doubt. You would like others to do this for you, so then do it for them.

Those in glass houses should not throw stones.

Having a clear conscience is priceless and we avoid many pitfalls when we live life cleanly. What does that mean? When we stay clean and clear in our words and actions, and when we honor the golden rule, then we build a shield around us called *integrity*. When you have integrity, people will feel your light because you are congruent with what you teach. You are authentic!

When you have integrity, there is no reason to hide or feel guilty. Challenges will still appear because that is part of life, but you can sleep at night because you know your words and your actions match.

If you would like to go deeper with the principles in this chapter see the appendix for practical exercises.

THE 7 HERMETIC PRINCIPLES

The Principle of Mentalism

The all is mind;
The universe is mental and
everything is a mental creation.

Consider where you see this principle in your life. How can you use this principle to help you as you navigate life?

CHAPTER 6

ASK FOR HELP

As you may already know, or may be starting to see from what I have shared so far, there is a lot more to us and to our world than we can see. In our quest to **Know Thyself** and live a life of freedom, peace and joy we have many allies – some who you might never have thought of before. There are invisible beings upon whom we can call. You might not be able to see these beings with your physical eye, but they are there. When we discover the multidimensional nature of our existence, we realize that we have helpers all around – beings who are ready to become friends and start a mutually beneficial relationship with us. If you become friends with these beings, just like any human friend, they will start to work with you.

First of all, there are the angels, who can only help us if we *ask* because we have free will and they do not. You can always ask angels for help. There are innumerable angels there for every single thing that you could need – the angel of drawing, the angel of communication, the angel of fun, the angel of writing. Ask for help and you will receive it!

*Help will always be given at Hogwarts
to those who ask for it.*

J.K. Rowling, Harry Potter and the Deathly Hallows

Have you ever wondered why magickal creatures – dragons, fairies, unicorns, mermaids, etc – exist in the stories of every land and culture? Because they are real! They just live in a different dimension. Fairies, Elves, Dragons, Mermaids, Unicorns, Gnomes and Pegasus are not just myths. They exist and are waiting to reconnect with humans. The more you connect with the unseen, the more allies you have, the more support you have for a mutually beneficial outcome.

When I first started connecting with Dragons, I learned from one Dragon that he felt that they had been ignored. No one likes to be ignored – but it is more than preference – our emotions and thoughts change our reality. In the book, *Hidden Messages of Water,* Dr. Masuro Emoto shares his groundbreaking experiments that prove our thoughts and words have an effect on water – and since we are 70 percent water, our thoughts affect us.

In one of the experiments, Dr. Emoto writes the phrase *I love you* on one container of rice, and *I hate you* on another. A third one is tucked away hidden from view and is ignored. The rice with *I love you* has not deteriorated much – the rice with *I hate you* got black, but still had its form. The rice that was ignored became a black liquid. It shows that being ignored is worse than being hated. So if I want support from the Dragons, I will post a beautiful picture of a dragon to thank them.

Another way I work with the magickal beings is that I ask them to support my endeavors to bring light to humans. I tell them that if we are better and remember who we are, we will treat them better. It is a win/win! Also, I included this chapter in the book to honor them and their contribution to the world – and to me.

Everything is alive – everything is moving – even the mineral kingdom (see the Hermetic principle of vibration). Bodies of water have divas associated with them. Trees and plants have spirits. When I go to a body of water, I give an offering, or offer a prayer to the beings there. There are also elemental beings that are associated with water, earth, fire and air – the elements that make up our body. We have allies who can help us everywhere we go!

Of course some of the most helpful beings are other humans. Working with a human team will get you to your goals more quickly. The team approach uses time efficiently and creates a powerful energy that could not be accomplished solo. I love to work with a team because it is more fun, and I am not good at everything. Others have special God given gifts that I do not have. I love to let others shine in their roles. It is a powerful blessing to work together for a common goal. The common goal of the team I am on, the Modern Mystery School, is Shamballah or peace on Earth – for *all* beings, not just us humans. What could be better?

Ask, and it will be given to you;
seek, and you will find; knock,
and it will be opened to you.
Matthew 7:7

HONOR YOUR BODY TEMPLE

Once we understand that there are spirits connected to all plants, we will look at the use of plant medicine differently. When we are stressed, we may turn to plant medicine as a way to cope or escape. If we are sensitive, it may be hard to be grounded in our body. Therefore, we may use plant medicine or other recreational drugs. I experienced this, and I will share that story.

Marijuana is very popular now because it is legal. Calling it plant medicine can make it seem fine to do. But there is more to the story. These plants have been altered and modified so much that the essence of the plant and its original purpose has been lost. These plants have been defiled with widespread abuse. There is always an energy exchange.

When you use plant medicine, you receive something from the plant temporarily (being high and maybe feeling elated), but the spirit of the plant is also taking something from you, a piece of you.

I know this to be true because in the past I used drugs to escape my pain. I smoked pot for five years when I was in college after my date rape experience. I used it to medicate myself and I loved it. I liked the smell and the taste. I liked how it made me feel. I bonded with people through it. But using pot robbed me of my passion and prolonged the issue I was trying to escape. I felt fried and I became apathetic. When you are around someone who smokes pot often, you will notice that they are foggy, confused or lackluster and their energy is as well. The term *burnout* is used for good reason.

Once I found the Mystery School I was able to stop using pot and alcohol. I learned powerful lineage rituals that surrounded me with light and protection, and gave me a way to call in allies and assistance. I was also able to discern what issues were mine and what issues belonged to others. With these powerful tools I have been able to progress on my spiritual path, and I have found ways to feel a high that is even better than any I experience with drug use – and there is no hangover. I have learned that we can get high off of our own energy field and through spiritual progression.

To repair the damage I did from my years of drug use I went through a 10-session series called the Spiritual Drug Detox. Until I received that, I could feel that my energy field had been damaged. Right after completing this healing series I was able to attract a higher caliber of student. Before receiving the series, it was almost as if people could sense that energetically I could not take them to the next level until I received the healing series.

What I share here with you about plant medicine comes from my direct personal experience. While training as a Universal Kabbalah Apprentice Teacher I had an experience that highlighted the damage I had inflicted on my soul and energy system as a result of my drug use. To become a Kabbalah Teacher one must go through a vetting process that is intensive because of the holiness and responsibility it entails. I was in the process of building a class to co-teach for the first time and not many students were signing up. Those who did were not really committed. The class ended up fizzling and I had to cancel it.

Around the same time, the training to offer the Spiritual Drug Detox healing series as a practitioner was offered (which I had received as a client to help me heal). I love taking classes in The Modern Mystery School and had signed up for most classes over the years with little resistance. But I had a lot of resistance to this class. Resistance is usually a sign that one is going to get a lot out of something. It means there is a block to overcome. The training class almost filled up before I paid my deposit, but I did finally sign up and take the class.

Receiving and training to give the Spiritual Drug Detox healing series restored my energy system and healed the damage that drug use had done to me. The next time I tried to build a Universal Kabbalah class, I was successful and it happened quickly. We are all psychic, and the students could sense I was solid and up to the task, hence on an unconscious or subconscious level they felt safe with me. This experience showed me how much we are damaging ourselves with the use of plant medicine.

The principle of vibration comes into play here. With my energy body restored my vibration became higher and attracted more serious and solid students to me.

No problem can be solved from
the same level of consciousness that created it.
Albert Einstein

Remember how at the beginning I told you that you might be triggered? Well here is a spot where that might happen. I also want to caution you about the use of ayahuasca. Anytime I work with someone that has done a lot of it, they have a vacant or spaced out stare; and if I warn them about using the drug they will become defensive. It is almost like the plant has melded to the person's energy field and is defending its right to be there. I have had a few people stop receiving healings or taking classes because they asked about ayahuasca and I was honest about it. I feel it is my *duty to* warn you, even though if you have used it you are likely to strongly reject this view.

If you find yourself wanting to disassociate and leave your body, you need to heal the cause. I found that the Mystery School healings and tools are very efficient. Energy clearing includes a Negative Energy Removal and an Emotional Cord Cutting that can help you feel much lighter and more joyful. The Life Activation will balance all your energy structures and light up the codons where your DNA lives. This activates your divine blueprint and helps you step into your purpose more fully. You can find a Mystery School practitioner anywhere in the world https://www.modernmysteryschoolint. com/certified-professionals/. Receiving the Empower Thyself initiation will give you rituals that will help you protect your energy field. Classes like Sacred Geometry will teach you how to create a clean energy space in your home or office. These are all ways to feel safe so that you actually want to be in your body. I have found them to be much more effective than plant medicine, without the negative side effects.

I also recommend deep body work like Hellerwork or Rolfing to help you get into your body as it will help remove stuck energy and increase your vibration. These modalities help erase stored trauma and make it easier to stay grounded and present. I have seen people heal very quickly and increase their awareness of when to put up boundaries in the moment.

If you would like to go deeper with the principles in this chapter see the appendix for practical exercises.

THE 7 HERMETIC PRINCIPLES

The Principle of Vibration

Nothing rests;
everything moves;
everything vibrates.
Even things that appear to be solid are vibrating.
If you control your own mental vibrations
you can align with the good of all.

Consider where you see this principle in your life. How can you use this principle to help you as you navigate life?

If God Lives in you and is a part of you
then you have the obligation to
walk the Earth as a God or Goddess.

CHAPTER 7

LIVE A ROYAL LIFE

Your job on earth is to remember who you are. You are an eternal being, a divine being, a royal being. Living life as a royal being is simply reclaiming your birthright. What does it mean to live a royal life? How does a king or a queen live? They live by caring for those in their charge. They devote themselves to a life of service. When you remember this, you are a shining beacon of light for yourself and for others around you. We all gain when we raise the bar. You are me and I am you.

Living a royal life is a new concept to most people. Many live by taking baby steps down a prescribed path, or within an invisible box, without much thought. It is like going 1, 2, 3, 4, 5, 6, 7, 8, 9. This is safe, but it is also mediocre. We are meant to expand exponentially – continually.

I like to live according to the Fibonacci sequence. This idea comes from one of my teachers, Founder Gudni Gudnason who opened the Modern Mystery School to the public in 1997. The Fibonacci sequence goes 0, 1, 1, 2, 3, 5, 8, 13, 21, 34 and so on. It starts out slowly and then the gap between numbers gets larger and larger, representing leaps – each greater than the one before! Starting at 1, 1, 2 (1+1), 3 (1+2), little steps, 5 (2+3), a little leap, 8 (3+5), a bigger leap, 13 (5+8), a bigger leap, 21 (8+13) an even bigger leap. This is the proper flow of the God human.

Let me explain these leaps in a practical way. I recently trained for a 5k (I have not run any distance since I was 12). I started very slowly – walking a few minutes then running one minute for a few rounds. The next day I did about the same. The next couple of days I did a little more. Then I made a leap to 10 minutes running and 3 minutes walking, and 10 more minutes walking. Then I went to two sets of 15 minutes of running, until within 8 weeks I ran 30 minutes non stop. Each leap built on the foundation before it.

The greatest risk is not taking a risk.

This is a simple example, but it applies to everything. Running was scary for me, but now I am running 30 minutes a day! The unknown can be frightening – but then you do it and feel so good about yourself. I just started learning pickleball and was nervous the first day of class, but felt so accomplished after going. I had many reasons why I could miss it, but pushed through. Eventually I will be good at this new skill and it will open opportunities for me to meet new people.

This can be done with larger goals too. I used to be scared to teach Empower Thyself; now I do it easily. That led me to train to become a Kabbalah teacher, which is even more responsibility. It took me 9 years to move from being an apprentice teacher to a full teacher. This weekend I have a class of 38 people and I am not nervous at all.

Living as a God means you leap; and where you land when you leap becomes the platform for the next leap!

The God human leaps.

We are meant to leap because we are eternal beings. We have never been born, therefore we can never die. So there's really nothing to fear. We limit ourselves because of the blockages in our subconscious. If you start to leap, then leap again, and yet again, you may be uncomfortable, but guess what? We are NOT meant to be comfortable!

Think of where you can go with leaps instead of steps. With the Fibonacci way of life you are not in your comfort zone; but every time you leap, you realize how good it feels. Have you ever done something that you've been afraid to do? If you put a lot of energy into it, you actually accomplish it. Then you end up thinking, *Oh my gosh, I'm so glad I did that – it was a challenge but I did it.* Then this higher platform of performance in life becomes your next baseline – a higher foundation. From there you are ready for the next leap. You start to ask, *What is the next goal?* That's what living by the Fibonacci sequence feels like.

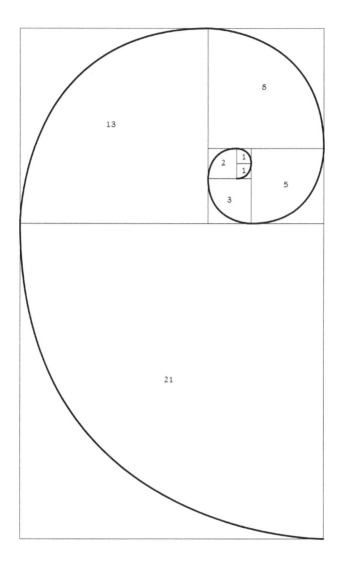

Magick and breakthroughs happen
outside of your comfort zone.
Through repeated practice,
magick becomes second nature.

Dr. Theresa Bullard
Ipsissima in the Lineage of King Salomon

Here is an example to help you understand this approach to life. Imagine you are about to jump off a high dive or a cliff. Your mind is saying, *This is impossible. I shouldn't do this. This is not safe.* Your legs are shaking, you're scared, and your mind is stopping you. It's uncomfortable; but then you decide to just jump into a pool of water. You jump, and you find that it was not that bad. You discover that it was actually fun! You might even say, *I want to go again and maybe I want to start higher.*

That is the Fibonacci way. It is about not letting fear stop you. It is starting with small steps and working your way up to larger steps. I've practiced this constantly. I used to be very uncomfortable *in my skin*. I was afraid of being in front of people. But then I started taking small steps. I led meditation – and then taught small classes. Now I teach a Universal Kabbalah class with 50 people in it.

If I had let myself stop at teaching three people, or decided that I did not want to challenge myself – feeling that discomfort – then I would not have grown. Then the people that I am meant to serve would not have grown.

MAKING MISTAKES

Many of us are afraid to make mistakes. It is actually better to live and make mistakes than to sit on your couch – at least you are learning. Making mistakes is a part of life. We don't punish a child for falling when they are learning to walk, so why be harsh on yourself as you try something new? (Chapter 3 can help with this issue.)

How do you know how far you can go until you have gone too far? I have found that each time I try something new and say *yes* to life, I learn important lessons – especially from the mistakes I make. That gives me direct personal experience that will help me in the future. Nothing has ever been wasted. All experience is useful.

MEDIOCRITY

Watch out for mediocrity. It keeps you with the crowd. It keeps you in a perception of safety because you're not risking anything. You cannot really fail because you're not trying to achieve anything. And yet, you ultimately fail even more than if you had tried. I learned that when I take a risk and fail, I still feel brave. Because of that, I respect myself even more. In these situations, I know that I have lived on this earth's playground as a God and not a coward. I have tested something new! From here I can branch out from that gained awareness. I win!

One of my favorite things to read is *The Man in the Arena* by Theodore Roosevelt. It inspires me. I have a great deal of respect for those who put themselves out there. Yes, maybe they make mistakes; but they are *brave*. I would rather risk falling on my face than hold back. So many people have opinions about everything. They hide behind a computer screen criticizing books, movies, art, plays, or a business on Yelp. I always wonder, *Why don't you go out and create something?* See how the following inspires you.

The Man in the Arena

It is not the critic who counts;
not the man who points out
how the strong man stumbles,
or where the doer of deeds could have done them better.
The credit belongs to the man who is actually in the arena,
whose face is marred by dust and sweat and blood;
who strives valiantly; who errs,
who comes short again and again,
because there is no effort without error and shortcoming;
but who does actually strive to do the deeds;
who knows great enthusiasms, the great devotions;
who spends himself in a worthy cause;
who at the best knows
in the end the triumph of high achievement,
and who at the worst, if he fails,
at least fails while daring greatly,
so that his place shall never be
with those cold and timid souls
who neither know victory nor defeat.

—Theodore Roosevelt

BE OF SERVICE

One way to really live life is to be of service! To truly live a royal life, one must be of service, true service, to others. The highest service that I have fulfilled is to help others remember who they truly are as divine beings. The Mystery School tradition trains us in the authentic acknowledgement, confirmation, and affirmation that someone is God. As a Guide in the Lineage of King Salomon, it is my job to help others transform by remembering their divine nature. Why is this? If you do not know your divine nature, it is easy for you to be a victim and blame others for your problems. But if you realize your divine nature and live a royal life based on your individuality (not your personality), you can live a life of joy, and serve as an example to inspire others to do the same.

Some people do not like the word service because they think of it as being a servant (or a slave). This is not true at all. I have realized through experience that the best way to know myself is through service to others. And as we said at the beginning, the goal of life is to **Know Thyself**. When you serve another, you will know yourself because everyone is actually a reflection of you! We all are one, and so helping another person's progress actually will help you progress, too.

In the process of coming to know yourself, may you see that you are Eternal, Divine and Royal. May you live as an Eternal, Divine and Royal being in every moment of your life.

THE 7 HERMETIC PRINCIPLES

The Principle of Gender

Gender is in everything;
everything has its masculine and feminine principles;
gender manifests on all planes.
Like the Yin and Yang everything has Male and Female.
We need both masculine (force)
and feminine (form) to create anything.

Consider where you see this principle in your life. How can you use this principle to help you as you navigate life?

You never know how far you can go,

until you go too far.

T.S Elliot

CONCLUSION
CREATE YOUR WORLD

Once you **Know Thyself**, find and clear your triggers, and align with the will of God, you can create your world. You have actually been creating your world all along; but now you can create more intentionally and more effectively to be in alignment with your highest desires.

Quantum physics is now proving what the mystery schools have known all along: we are divine creator beings. Quantum physics proves this with wave and particle experiments. Everything is a wave until a human puts their awareness on that wave. Then it becomes a particle. This means that our focus will shift the material world around us. In physics, everything has unlimited potential. A wave has within it endless potential of what it can manifest. If a human causes the wave to become a particle that human actually shifts reality. We are creators.

As creator gods, if we focus on a positive outcome, we can shift the world outside us more quickly. Shamballah, or Peace on Earth, is the mission of my lineage! To achieve this, we first create peace within us, which is then reflected in the world. Everything is a mirror of us. I learned the hard way to avoid the pitfalls of focusing on problems outside myself – like environmental issues. Yes, it is important to look out for our fellow humans and for our environment; but the quickest way to solve these issues is to know ourselves. If we clean up our thoughts, the rivers will be clean. When we reconcile pollution in our inner world, we will see pollution disappear in the outer world. When we end the war within us, we will find peace in the world. As we know from Hermetics: As within, so without.

My intention in *Spiritual Shortcuts* is to help you see that you have the power to shift your outer world if you do the inner work. Life can be fun and magickal! We are meant to be realized Gods on Earth, playing with the elements and creating peace and harmony – and ultimately living a life full of *joy*. I hope the tips and exercises here guide you to live a magickal life.

Acknowledgments

Thank you to my mom, Judy Wallace, and my dad, Bob Wallace, who have always supported me even though I dance to the beat of my own drum.

Thank you to Hierophant and Founder Gudni Gudnason, Sovereign Ipsissimus Dave Lanyon, and Sovereign Ipsissimus Hideto Nagatomi for holding the Lineage of King Salomon and keeping it pure.

And to Heather Davis Desrocher, my editor, for her fire and infinite patience; and to Lorieanne Tamayo who generously gave her time and made suggestions to improve the book. I am so grateful!

Finally, thank you to April O'Leary and the entire team at O'Leary Publishing for turning my vision into such a beautiful reality.

PRACTICAL APPLICATION

Exercises for Going Deeper

CHAPTER 1

Know Thyself

Everyone is a Mirror

This exercise will help you to take responsibility for your life!

1. Take out a piece of paper and think of a few people who trigger you.
2. Write down the qualities that they have that annoy you.
3. If you really cannot find someone who annoys you in your world, then use a public figure for this exercise. **Do not read ahead** – just write.
4. The annoying qualities you listed are qualities that *you* have but do not like about yourself. You have projected onto your outer world.
5. NOTE: For the difficult ones – if you choose, as an example, a child abuser, and you don't actually abuse children, you can look within at how you treat your own inner child. How do you beat up him or her?

CHAPTER 2

Find Your Buttons

The 15-Minute Rule

Your buttons or triggers can be keys to your power.

Learn to be joyous in finding the things that trigger you. At first many things will trigger you. But as you grow and clear them, fewer things will bother you – you may need to challenge yourself to find them.

When something triggers you, feel it head on. Then, you can investigate:

Is this a passing thing?

Do you need to express a boundary and then you can move on OR is it still bothering you after 15 minutes?

If it still bothers you after 15 minutes, then you know it is not current but from the past.

CHAPTER 3
FREE YOURSELF

How Old Am I?

Find photos of yourself as a child at various ages and keep them on your phone, or somewhere you can connect to them often.

When something triggers a negative reaction in you (especially if it is not gone in 15 minutes), ask yourself: *How old am I?* You will often find that you are reacting from a younger self.

Looking at the photos of you as a child may help. Once you know how old you are in this trigger, comfort your inner child. Let him or her know that you love them no matter what.

This will rewire your energy field. Eventually rejection from the outside will not bother you because you and yourself are *good*.

CHAPTER 4

BE AUTHENTIC

Do I Really Want to Go?

When you are invited to an event or to hang out with someone, notice your thoughts and feelings.

Are you reluctant to attend the event or hang out due to a negative feeling or trigger?

Will attending make you step out of your comfort zone into a growth zone?

If the answer to either of those questions is yes, then get honest with yourself and see if you are up for a challenge. If not, you are more self aware as a result of asking.

If the event sounds fun and you are into it – go. If you are saying *yes* out of obligation, it is best for all parties if you decline – as long as you are not avoiding out of fear. This is how I operate, and it creates an aura of integrity. People will trust you because you are in alignment!

The exception is if the event is for service. Sometimes there will be a natural resistance to the light, and we need to push through and get to the other side. In other words, only participate in agreements that are win/win for both parties.

CHAPTER 5

ALIGN WITH THE WILL OF GOD

Sacred Geometry Meditation

This is a way to use Sacred Geometry to manifest with your highest good.

1. Visualize a pyramid over your head (in Sacred Geometry the triangle or pyramid represents connection to Spirit).
2. Ask a question.
3. Visualize the answer rising up into the pyramid around your head.
4. You might sense, feel, see or hear the answer.
5. Then bring the answer into a cube that is from your shoulders to your hips. The answer can be refined in the upper part of the cube.
6. Now bring the answer into the lower part of the cube – the answer will start to take on the form of action.
7. Now visualize a sphere around your legs and feet.

Alternative: Pray each morning that your thoughts, words, and actions will all be in alignment with the will of God.

CHAPTER 6

ASK FOR HELP

Develop a Relationship with the Unseen

There are magickal beings everywhere! You can develop friendships with gnomes, fairies, elves, dragons, mermaids, etc. when you are open and earnest.

Open your mind to the unseen. Initiate connecting or communicating with these beings. For example, when you go to a river, talk to the Deva (the Spirit of the river) and listen. What do you hear back? You might receive guidance. Talk to the trees – the mountains. Give an offering! What to give? They will tell you what they want.

Ask the angels for support with projects, relationships, or anything else and see what happens.

CHAPTER 7

LIVE A ROYAL LIFE

Explore Royalty

Ask these questions to see what comes to you:

What does it mean to be Royal?

What is the archetype of a Queen or a King?

How does an aligned Queen and King hold themselves?

How do they present themselves?

How do they care for themselves?

How do they serve others?

Start to apply the answers to your own life.

GLOSSARY OF TERMS

Empower Thyself Initiation: The initiation happens at the end of a 2-day class. With initiation one is adopted into the lineage of King Salomon and receives 10 times the light to support your unique purpose, alignment with the will of God, four new Guides, and Divine protection into the light.

Evil: anything that stops the progression of the God Human

Guide: a title given to a leader in the Mystery School who can initiate people into the lineage

Hermetics: laws of Reality

Kabbalah: the study of the God Essence in humans. It is open to all regardless of your race, religion or belief system. It teaches how to create like God creates.

Life Activation: turns on the codes of your spiritual and physical DNA so you can achieve your God-given mission on Earth

Lineage: an unbroken lineage of teachings and knowledge that has been handed down from teacher to student in an oral tradition. (The lineage of King Salomon the Wise is one lineage.)

Magick: creating something from nothing or turning one thing into another thing

Metaphysics: the study of how spiritual energies manifest in the physical, or the marriage of spirituality and science

Mystery School: There are seven authentic, lineage-based ancient Mystery Schools on the planet. A Mystery School holds the flame of esoteric wisdom. When one is ready one will find the Mystery School.

Ritual: a way of calling in, holding and dismissing energy in a holy way

Trigger: Something unhealed within you that reacts when touched. We are only as strong as our weakest part.

About the Author

From a young age, Erin Wallace felt a desire to help the world. In high school, she was an activist who received the Beyond War award at the age of 16, and was on the cover of two magazines; she learned early on that anger and polarization did not create change. After a traumatic experience in college, Erin sought out spiritual solutions and dabbled in many paths – discovering what not to do. She was inspired by Quantum Physics, and loved how science proved what she felt, that our consciousness creates the material world.

After completing a year-and-a-half of Hellerwork Body-work Training in Australia, Erin met her destiny at a Holistic Fair where a healer with the Modern Mystery School talked about the 22-strand DNA Activation – now called the Life Activation. Since Erin attended Healer's Academy with the Mystery School she has not looked back.

Erin has dedicated her life to serving all beings on earth, including humans, and is a Universal Hermetic Ray Kabbalah Teacher, Leader of Modern Mystery School California, and a Certified Guide, Healer, and Teacher through the Modern Mystery School International. Her mission is to help create Shamballah, or heaven on earth, for all.

You can find Erin at erinkathleenwallace.com and also at modernmysteryschoolnorcal.com.

Printed in the USA
CPSIA information can be obtained
at www.ICGtesting.com
LVHW071929031023
760054LV00020B/454